# Lighting the Lamps

# Lighting *the* Lamps

*A Gift to Our Children*

*A Parent's Guide to Raising Responsible,
Loving Children in Today's World*

**EDNA GREEN**

Providence House Publishers
PROVIDENCE PUBLISHING CORPORATION
FRANKLIN, TENNESSEE

Permission is granted by the author to reproduce *My Special Thoughts* book pages and the provided charts to individualize your child's book or home school program.

Copyright 2004 by Edna Green

All rights reserved.

Printed in the United States of America

08    07    06    05    04    1    2    3    4    5

Library of Congress Control Number: 2003114818

ISBN: 1-57736-309-4

*Cover photo by Daniel H. Green*
*Cover design by Lindrel Moates*

Scripture quotations marked RSV are from the Revised Standard Version of the Bible, copyright 1952 [2nd edition, 1971] by the Division of Christian Education of the National Council of the Churches of Christ in the United States of America. Used by permission. All rights reserved.

Scripture quotations marked KJV are taken from the Holy Bible, King James Version, Cambridge, 1769.

PROVIDENCE HOUSE PUBLISHERS
an imprint of
Providence Publishing Corporation
238 Seaboard Lane • Franklin, Tennessee 37067
www.providence-publishing.com
800-321-5692

# Contents

| | |
|---|---|
| FOREWORD | vii |
| PREFACE | ix |
| ACKNOWLEDGMENTS | x |
| INTRODUCTION FOR PARENTS | 1 |
| PART 1. NURTURING AND INFLUENCING THE UNCONSCIOUS | 6 |
| PART 2. AFFECTING CONSCIOUS DECISION-MAKING SKILLS THROUGH LOVING FACILITATORS | 17 |
| COPY-READY MATERIALS | 27 |
|     MY SPECIAL THOUGHTS BOOK PAGES | 28 |
|     SECRET GARDEN FOLDER | 42 |
|     CHARTS AND POSTERS | 43 |
|       1. Wise Choice | 43 |
|       2. My Feelings | 44 |
|       3. Help Sheet | 45 |
|       4. Four Goals of Unwise Choices | 46 |
|       5. Special Wonderful Me | 47 |

| | | |
|---|---|---|
| 6. | Family Will For You | 48 |
| 7. | Wheel of Misery | 49 |
| 8. | The Good Life | 50 |
| 9. | Our Family Plan | 51 |
| 10. | Wonderful Person | 52 |
| 11. | God Made Me | 53 |

BIBLIOGRAPHY     54

# Foreword

Having worked with Edna Green's system as a social worker with metropolitan Nashville public schools, I thought it important to promote her ideas. I witnessed increased motivation from empowered students who viewed the teacher as "on their side" as a child-centered student advocate. I encouraged Edna to present her program at a meeting of social workers so that her ideas could be shared systemwide. Techniques were taken by principals, teachers, and social workers, and used with much success. I believe that this is not only an excellent system for appropriately addressing academic, social, and behavioral situations in the classroom, but also for preparing students for the larger society. My observations support my beliefs in this program's ability to make a positive impact in children's lives.

Dorothy Gasser Primm

# Preface

Twenty-five years ago I returned to the classroom from a year of study in elementary counseling. I attempted then to create ways of teaching children the basic elements of what I called "The Good Life."

The results were exciting and rewarding—not only were these children learning to make wise choices and to know that they were special, wonderful people, but many achieved higher than expected scores on their achievement tests.

Research in my classroom revealed that several academically challenged fourth graders had improved dramatically. The average Peabody Individual Achievement Test score for four of my lowest achieving students had improved two years and six months—in one year! Clearly, something special had happened.

What I describe to you could be called a teaching method, but I believe it is much more correct to call it a tried-and-true, life-giving, character-building communication system for the family.

As you weave these Christian thought patterns into your daily living and they become a way of life in your home, you will give your children "the abundant life," and you will instill in them an unconscious desire for loving, caring relationships. Thus, the whole family will become more understanding and loving.

In my later years, as I witness more heartwarming results with inner-city children, I am convinced that this "life-giving" communication system should be published so that future generations might benefit.

Enjoy and learn from my experience, and, along with me, continue to pursue the educating and loving of our children.

Edna Green

# Acknowledgments

The special people who helped and encouraged me through the years are *Dorothy Primm*, a social worker whose early encouragement and input kept me moving toward refining my goals; *Pat Mynatt*, a kindergarten teacher who encouraged me to adapt my materials for kindergarten use; *Joe Seibert*, my principal who cooperated in every way with my "new ideas" and allowed me to grow in my early days; *Kathryn W. Smith*, a friend from college days, without whose help I couldn't have finished putting this information together for publication; *Reverend Donna Scott Eley*, a priest who made me more aware of Carl Jung and offered suggestions, ideas, and support; *Keith Carlson*, a professor at Middle Tennessee State University who nurtured my understandings of counseling; *Edwin Conly*, a highly disciplined, wise priest who taught me so much about the faith; *Wes and Mark Green*, my sons who have helped me with accuracy and wording; *Thomas Green and Virginia Green*, my grandchildren who posed for my cover picture; and *Daniel H. Green*, my grandson who took the photograph on the cover.

# Introduction for Parents

We live in an uncertain world marked by violence, immorality, and uncivilized behavior of every sort. Sometimes we feel that our world is completely out of control. In such an environment, how can we nurture our children so that their hearts will embrace the good and virtuous life, a life that conforms to a standard of right? How can we encourage our children to construct a moral life for themselves so that they will reject the world of drugs and alcohol, of immorality and violence, and of evil intentions—even suicide—that eventually will adversely affect all their relationships and activities?

If the answer to preventing problems and troubled lives could be restricted to communicating with the rational, conscious mind, the problem could be easily solved. We could just make a list of all acceptable behaviors and then explain that they should not do otherwise, (as with Adam and Eve in the Garden of Eden, prohibit their eating the "forbidden fruits"), allowing them to emerge as God's perfect people.

This also is similar to the story of Noah and the Ark (Genesis 9:21–25), which tells of the attempt to select the good and destroy the evil, thus creating a perfect world. Of course, this scheme was doomed to failure. The Genesis story relates that soon after the flood, Noah became drunk with wine and his son mocked him; therefore, Noah placed a curse on him. Even efforts of such heroic magnitude were not successful in ridding the world of evil, so we have to acknowledge and deal with the presence of evil in our lives.

The book of Exodus abounds with extensive rules to guide people in living their lives in proper relationships; if these rules are followed in scrupulous detail, so the theory goes, evil would be powerless and all could live in harmony—a completely rational solution.(In fact, it sounds like part of a conscious plan that teachers and parents employ every day.) Unfortunately, however, the nature of humans is too complex for a set of laws. Since Old Testament times, people have acknowledged that we cannot obey laws; we simply cannot "be good."

It follows that we cannot tell our children to "be good" and expect them not to do wrong again. Perhaps we are up against the problem of original sin, described by some church scholars as a weakness of the will leading to sin. You will recall what Saint Paul said in Romans 7:15–19:

> I do not understand my own actions. For I do not do what I want but I do the very thing I hate.... I can will what is right, but I cannot do it. For I do not do the good I want but the evil I do not want is what I do. (RSV)

We are forced to ask whether the source of people's behavior is conscious or unconscious, or perhaps a combination of both. I surmise that the unconscious mind, with its strong hidden agendas from early childhood, becomes the crucible in which conscious and unconscious decisions in life materialize. Most of us are not aware of our deepest motives, our hidden agendas. We must wonder how these agendas became such ruling forces in our lives, powerfully directing our choices and actions unbeknownst to us.

Can we get a handle on the kinds of experiences that influence the contents of our unconscious minds, thus determining our hidden agendas? How do we attempt to form a healthy unconscious in our children, since that appears to be the matrix for the formation of the core self and ultimately the God-self?

Morton Kelsey states in *Discernment* that "children need to know that there are two different worlds: physical and spiritual.... They can be trained so they are open to relating to God as love at the center of reality or closed to this idea because of the way that human beings have treated them." In *The Better Part*, noted Catholic lecturer and leader of the Centering Prayer movement Thomas Keating says:

> There are three basic energy centers of the human organism. These develop out of the instinctual needs of every infant for [1] security and survival, [2] affection and esteem, and [3] power and control. These are biological necessities. But when they are withheld, we either develop compensatory attitudes or repress the painful frustrations of those needs into the unconscious. There, the energy remains, *secretly* influencing our behavior and our decision-making process.

According to Keating, "The real source of most of our emotional problems actually is the fragility of early childhood." If we parents, teachers, and other adults wish to affect a child's source of behavior, we must focus, as much as we are able, on the deepest level of functioning, both conscious and unconscious.

Renowned theologian and author John Sanford in *Healing Body and Soul* speaks of the direct relationship between sin and unconsciousness:

> To be unconscious, to be in the dark, or lacking insight into oneself and the circumstances of life, means that we will inevitably miss the mark and thus will sin . . . sin can ultimately be overcome only with the increase of consciousness. Sin and unconsciousness are inseparable, the one always existing with the other. . . . Therefore, only insofar as we pursue a life dedicated to self-knowledge and illumination, can we hope to avert some of the effects of sin.

Our purpose is to help in building within our children the healthiest core self (with its agendas) possible, so that the inner being is not working against itself, but will always be moving toward the good and virtuous life with purpose: to love oneself as well as others, to love God and care about His world—all reinforced with faith, hope, trust, expectation, and gratitude. What a gift to our children and the world if we could light the lamps of self-understanding so that as they experience life now and in the future, they can have insight and continued growth; so that they can and will become more and more what God would have them be.

In *Compassion and Self-Hate,* Theodore Rubin states, "Each of us contains two opposing forces of enormous power and effect. Compassion is the strongest human therapeutic agent in existence. Its potential for constructive growth and human creative possibility is almost limitless. Self-hate is the strongest human antitherapeutic agent in existence. Its potential for destructive possibility is almost limitless. . . . There is no question that the self-hating autonomy is a totalitarian slave master." We cannot ignore the fact that abusive, non-caring, unloving treatment will produce problem children—children plagued with feelings of self-doubt, anger, fear, revenge, guilt, depression, despair, excessive attention needs, and general unhappiness and restlessness.

What kinds of behavior can we expect from the unfortunate recipients of abuse and neglect? We can count on it: they will gravitate toward drugs and alcohol as well as various other compulsive behaviors as ways to kill the pain or to compensate. In general they will tend to display anger, violence, immorality, and an array of self-defeating and self-hating behaviors. Needless to say, they will choose friends who have similar feelings and problems; they may even join gangs. These hurting young adults will lack the ability to love and accept themselves or any other individuals, thus making them unsuitable as marriage partners—relationships most likely doomed to failure. In their lack of understanding their painful lives, they could despair and become withdrawn or even suicidal.

Keating says of all children that "the unconscious motivation is firmly in place by the age of three or four, and more deeply entrenched by the age of reason." We remember little or nothing of what occurs in our lives before the age of four, but the emotional impact of these occurrences shapes the foundation of our unconscious. Mothers and fathers especially need to take very seriously the importance of these first four years. Keating further notes that "the more we were damaged as children by inconsiderate treatment, the greater our compensatory needs and the more firmly our emotional programs are likely to be in place."

We cannot control the environment in which our children will be living, but we can connect them to a deep, wise, and dependable inner strength that will serve them well in any environment. As with the flood story and other biblical references, we, with our conscious plans and efforts, will be unable to control and direct our children's behaviors. Simply put, we cannot coerce them into the virtuous, loving life with preaching, controlling rules, and threats of severe punishments. Our most effective role will be that of a *loving facilitator*.

Carl Jung powerfully states, "Acceptance of oneself is the essence of the moral problem and the acid test of one's whole outlook on life." The answer to our dilemma has to be love, for God is love. Children must know that God loves them and that He created them to love them forever—unconditional love.

Basic for parents, teachers, and children:
- Love God and His world
- Love and accept yourself *with* all your imperfections (not *after* you get rid of all your faults)
- Love your spouse (including faults)
- Love your children and family (with all their faults)
- Love your neighbors (with all their faults)

. . . all with appreciation and without reservation. This is the environment in which our children can grow toward the virtuous life and become the loving people God would have them be.

We are unable to make fair judgments on others since we don't know the content of their unconscious and their problems in life. Hope for our enemies lies in loving them in spite of their behaviors. How are we poor souls to pour out all of this perfect love in view of the fact that we, too, have had a few "fragile" experiences along life's way? We may not have joined a gang or committed suicide, but chances are we are living out varying degrees of aggression, self-criticism, and anxiety. Perhaps a little spark of evil has been fermenting within our unconscious for years, or maybe many sparks over many years?

It is logical to say that if inconsiderate, abusive, and unloving treatment causes children to repress painful experiences and live troubled lives, then considerate, accepting, respectful, loving treatment will facilitate their ability to love and accept themselves (without the need to repress extremely painful experiences), thus making the choice of the virtuous life much more likely, if not automatic.

If our children are to have the spiritual courage, emotional health, and wisdom they need to make godly choices and form loving relationships, it is essential that we not only love and accept them, but that we light the lamps of self-understanding at the earliest age. In the pages that follow, you'll discover a life-giving communication system that does just that, addressing both conscious and unconscious needs. Part one is designed to influence the unconscious in forming a healthy self-acceptance, while part two helps children with their conscious decision-making skills.

# Part 1

# Nurturing and Influencing the Unconscious

## BIRTH THROUGH FOUR YEARS

- Breast-feed if at all possible.
- Talk to the child, saying often:
    "Mother and Daddy love you."
    "Sister/brother loves you."
    "Grandmother and Granddaddy love you."
    "God loves you."
    "You are our wonderful baby/little girl/little boy."
    "God, who made the whole world, loves you very much. You are special to Him."
- Place picture of child with his/her mother and father in his/her room; also use pictures of other family members with the child.
- Place a poster on the wall with a picture of the smiling child on it, along with the words "Mother and Daddy love you" and "God loves you."
- If the child is in day care:
    Display the child's family picture (child with parents and siblings) on the wall, and under the picture, "Mother and Daddy love you." Every child in a day care room should be able to view his/her family picture all day.
- Demonstrate care and respect for each other in the child's presence. Say "Hello, you wonderful person, I love you" or "We all love you."
- At times of misbehavior, state for the child who is old enough to talk and understand:
    "You are choosing to (put paint on Mary's picture) and that is causing (her to feel hurt and angry)."
    "What can you do to help things go better?"
    "Remember, we all love you."

- Read fairy tales. Very young children cannot yet verbalize their deepest knowledge, but they can identify with the characters in the stories. Certain symbols and characters may attract them and help in value identification. John Sanford says that typical patterns underlying human life are depicted in this universal story form (bad gnome, good fairy, etc.)
- Discuss with children their dreams and visions. This will stimulate a deeper self-knowledge and help them validate and trust their intuitions.
- Help the child depict these ideas/concepts creatively through use of visible, tangible objects. Drawing fairy tale characters, places, and things remembered from dreams, and having these portrayals valued by parent or teacher, encourages the child's self-expression and provides an outlet for feeling responses too profound for words. A child can be encouraged to choose from already created objects or opt to make them in clay, providing opportunities to identify objects important to him/her. Even without symbol-making capacity, a child may be drawn to certain objects for reasons not fully understood. Treating the child's creations with respect validates his autonomy as a separate person who is permitted to initiate, explore, and question.

# FOUR YEARS THROUGH EIGHT YEARS

## My Special Thoughts Book

Make your child's book by copying pages in the back of this book [*pages 28-41*]. Choose only those pages that are appropriate for your child. Copy the pages and make them into your child's book. Put his/her name on the front cover and place pictures in the appropriate rectangles. Familiarize your child with his/her book at age four.

Read *My Special Thoughts* each day, then weekly beginning in the early conscious years (five years), and reinforce at every opportunity. The growing realization of being loved by God, by family, and by teachers becomes an unconscious force in the depth of his/her being for self-acceptance and for choosing love of self and neighbor. This support system should generate a lifelong impetus for choosing the virtuous life.

Remember that the guiding force in his/her life will be weighted heavily in the unconscious. His/her automatic behavior choices of later years will be rooted right here, so make these early years powerful with love and acceptance.

Your window of opportunity for input into the unconscious will dissipate as peer pressures begin to dominate the conscious mind and the child is actively processing life's experiences. The content of *My Special Thoughts* teaches the child to be aware of his/her feelings—how to listen to and respond to them—thus gaining valuable insight into self-understanding and skills for decision-making. Also, it gives him/her a permanent measuring stick (wise choice) for evaluating every behavior choice.

This should instill a just sense of responsibility for his/her choices of behavior and provide him/her with the courage to pursue the virtuous life with a sense of divine help.

### *How to Use the My Special Thoughts Book*

Before reading the booklet, say, "Relax your body and let your mind be at peace. Now think back millions of years ago when God began creating His special wonderful people. Your great-great-grandparents and their grandparents were there, and the plan for you was in the mix. Finally, after all these years, your grandparents and then your parents were born (all were/are God's special people). Then in the year _____ all of this creation came together in such a way that YOU were born (God's special, wonderful YOU). In His divine wisdom, God sent you at this time in history and in this place on earth with a plan and purpose. He made you to love you forever. You cannot do anything that will keep God from loving you. Even with your many unwise choices, He loves you.

"Now while you are being loved every moment of every day, you still are free to make your own choices in life. What you want to work on, with God's help, is to make the wisest choices that you are able to make, so that you can become all that God wants you to be."

Remember to emphasize that you are talking about the God who made the whole world —that thousands of years ago, God was making ready the time and place for him/her to be born on earth as a very special person—and God has a plan for him/her.

Keep in mind that the child is wonderful—meaning *full of wonder*. Who knows what God has prepared for your child? Parents, never forget the "specialness" of your child. Treat him/her with great respect and love and let God, with His infinite wisdom, and His angels direct your child on the path that only this child will take.

Read pages 28 through 35 (or pages appropriate to your situation). Say, "Making wise choices is what we want to do. How do we know what is wise?" Read, "I am wise . . ." on page 36.

Now say, "God gave me feelings to make life interesting and these feelings guide me through life. They let me know when things just aren't right as well as when they seem to be right." If you have ever seen anyone who seems to have no feelings—simply not able to feel—then you will know how wonderful it is that we all have our feelings. Thanks be to God!

"If your feelings are ever hurting so much that they are really getting to you—so painful that you are losing your ability to live life, then find a wise person (a minister, a priest, a counselor, a dependable family member) and ask for help." Read, "I know my feelings . . ." on page 37. This is a perfect time for the child to tell you or the counselor about his/her feelings.

**My Special Thoughts**

Child's Name

*picture of child's face*

page 28

---

Mother
and
Daddy
love me.

*picture of child with parents*

page 29

---

Mother
loves
me.

*picture of child with mother*

page 30

---

Grandmother
and
Granddaddy
love me.

*picture of child with grandparents*

page 31

---

_____ loves me.

*picture of child with other*

page 32

---

_____ and _____ love me.

*picture of child with others*

page 33

---

God made me to be His special, wonderful person. He will love me forever.

*picture of child*

page 34

---

God gave me intelligence so I can know His truth. I can know wise from unwise.

*picture of child pointing to head (intelligence)*

page 35

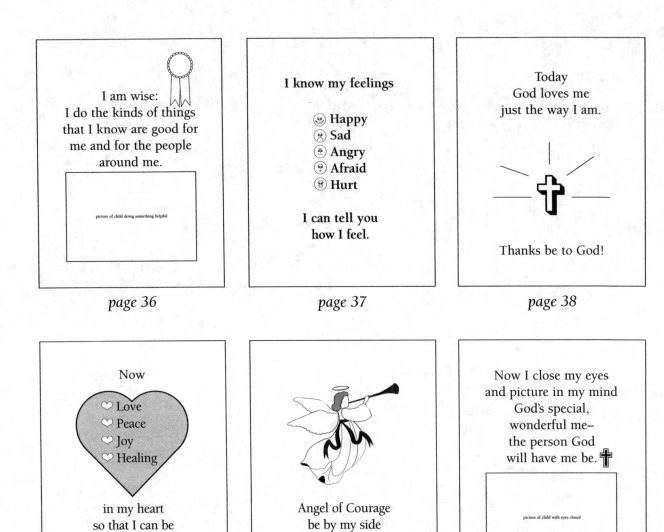

- Now read page 38.
- Say, "Place your hand on your heart while we read these pages."
  Then read pages 39 and 40.
- Finally, read page 41.

# The Wonderful Person Bulletin Board

Prepare a bulletin board with "Wonderful Person" in the center [*page 52*]. Choose a member of the family each week to be the "Wonderful Person" of the week. Remember, he/she doesn't earn this; he/she simply is God's special, wonderful person. Put the name at the top with a drawing or picture of the family member. Allow him/her to put items or pictures that are special to him/her (a picture of his/her pet, a favorite book, toy, etc.), along with words to describe what sort of person he/she would like to be. During that week, have all the other family members watch the wonderful person and whenever they see him/her making a wise choice, make a note about the wise choice and put it on the bulletin board. At the end of the week take a picture of the "Wonderful Person" standing by his/her special bulletin board with all the wonderful choices that were observed by family members that week. Then put all the items from the bulletin board along with the picture into a sack or folder for him/her to keep—a very special keepsake. During that week the "Wonderful Person" will have special treatment in the home.

Occasionally you will have a child who will say something like, "Well, he doesn't ever make any wise choices." Your response should be, "We are not focusing on unwise choices. All of us make those, but we are looking for wise choices, such as how he helps his friend or answers the phone, etc. You want to watch for wise choices."

11

## DEMONSTRATE YOUR LOVE

Both Mother and Father:
- Inundate your child with love, hugs, and kisses.
- Say regularly:

    "I love you."

    "You are our special wonderful child."

    "God, who made the whole world, loves you very much."

    "You are God's special wonderful person. He will always love you, even when you are making unwise choices."

    "Sister loves you." or "Brother loves you."

    "We all love you."

All of these words have little meaning if actions are inconsistent, so make sure that your child knows that he/she is loved—by your actions.

## SECRET GARDEN EXPERIENCE

Make a wall bulletin board by creating these posters. Place them where they are clearly visible:

*Poster #1*

God made me to be
His special, wonderful
person. He will love
me forever.

- Pictures of all family (or class) members attached to a large red heart.
- Attach the red heart with pictures to the bottom of this poster.
- Read poster # 1 together. Say, "Remember that God (who made the whole world) loves

you even when you make unwise choices. There is nothing that you can do that will keep him from loving you. There may be times when you are not loving yourself—when you are choosing to hurt yourself and others with unwise choices—but God keeps on loving you."

*Poster #2*

> **MY FEELINGS**
>
> He gave me feelings
> 1. Happy
> 2. Sad
> 3. Angry
> 4. Afraid
> 5. Hurt
>
> I feel_____
> because I_____.

- Read poster # 2. You might want to tell them that some people are so hurt in life that they finally have little ability to feel. "How lucky we are to be able to feel. Thanks be to God." When talking about feelings, always say, "I feel _____ because I _____." Don't say "I feel _____ because somebody else did/said something." Tell the child you want him/her to word his/her statement so that he/she is in charge of his/her feelings rather than someone else.

*Poster #3*

> God gave me intelligence
> so I can know wise
> from unwise.
> I can know what
> is good for me
> and for the people
> around me.

*Poster #4*

> He gave me Jesus in
> my heart to pour out
> - Love
> - Peace
> - Joy
> - Healing
>
> so that I can be
> the person
> God wants me to be.

- Say poster # 3 together.

- Now say together poster # 4.

13

"We have a secret garden, a secret spot deep within us—a place where we can go with our feelings and thoughts and no one else can come. We can go there to receive God's love—to talk to Jesus who is perfect love. Ask Jesus to be present with you in your garden. Remember He loves you with all your imperfections. He will love you forever. Make your garden grow with many loving thoughts. Ask for courage to put away unpleasant memories. Think of how much Jesus loves you. He has given you food, a place to live protected from bad weather, clothes to wear, parents (or *a parent*) who love and care for you, brothers and sisters, grandparents, friends, and teachers who care.

*Poster #5*

May the Angel of Courage take my hand.

"Thus, love, peace, joy, and healing of all hurts in my garden—in my heart. Thanks be to God. May the angel of courage take my hand."

*For Girls*

Give each girl a Secret Garden necklace (red heart for love, light blue heart for peace, yellow heart for joy, green heart for healing, and a small "angel of courage"). If you belong to a church that blesses items for God's use, have the necklace blessed. Let her know that it is a special item for a special purpose. Have the child wear the necklace so she can say the simple little request for help in times of hurt, anger, fear, or sadness by touching each heart and/or the angel.

- Touch the red heart and think about how much you are loved by Jesus. Say "love."
- Then touch the blue heart and try to think of peaceful feelings—the peace that God wants you to have. Say "peace."
- Touch the yellow heart and think of joy and happiness because you are loved. Say "joy."
- Touch the green heart and say, "Healing from all my hurts and fears. Thank you, Jesus."
- Touch the angel of courage and say, "Angel of Courage, help me. Take my hand."

No one will know what she is saying or inferring except the child. This is a tangible help when dealing with unpleasant experiences or feelings that confront happiness, and provides a spiritual connection with Jesus.

So, many times during the day, the child can say, "Love, peace, joy, and healing in my heart. Thanks be to God. May the Angel of Courage take my hand."

## Secret Garden Folder

You can also make folders for boys and girls using 14" x 8.5" paper divided into three parts or make an 8.5" x 11" folder using the chart provided in the back [*page 42*]. Print or glue these two sides back to back to make the booklet.

# Part 2

# Affecting Conscious Decision-Making Skills through Loving Facilitators

Teach children how to make wise choices. Provide them with the necessary structure and skills: tools, knowledge, understanding, and practice for making wise, conscious decisions each day and throughout life. Train them to think of their choices as being either wise or unwise—not good or bad, as you want to create a loving, accepting environment early in life in which they can experiment with decision-making without judgment or fear of punishment. This helps them gain knowledge, insight, and wisdom concerning their choices of behavior, and grow in confidence and self-acceptance.

Experiencing daily behavior choices under the guidance of a knowledgeable, loving facilitator provides the perfect setting for learning to make wise choices.

## WISE CHOICE CHART

Incorporate the following routine into the child's everyday experiences. This chart is the focus of every choice the child will make.

Say, "How can we all have the best day possible?"

Look at the Wise Choice chart [*page 43*]. After some discussion, conclude that if all of us in our family choose to "do the kinds of things that are good for us and for the people around us," we will have a good day. We all will agree.

> **WISE CHOICE**
>
> I do the kinds of things that I know are good for me and for the people around me.

Also remind your children that they are God's special, wonderful people. Thus they will want to do the kinds of things that will help them to become all that God made them to be: academically, socially, physically, emotionally, and spiritually.

They will want to help each other become all that they can become. So help, encourage, love, and respect each other. God made us all.

# MY FEELINGS CHART

**MY FEELINGS**

He gave me feelings
1. Happy
2. Sad
3. Angry
4. Afraid
5. Hurt

I feel_____
because I_____

Every child needs to know his/her feelings and be able to express those feelings in an accepting environment.

Place this chart [*page 44*] in clear view.

Not only will you check in on feelings with your children each morning, but you will refer to this chart whenever strong feelings emerge.

You will say to the child, "You feel _____ because you _____."

Ask, "Can you think of any choice that you can make that might help you to feel more the way you would like to feel?"

It is important that the child learn to structure his/her feelings in such a way that he/she is in charge of those feelings—not someone else or the world.

As his/her facilitator, you want to be as nonjudgmental as possible. Feelings have great influence on the choices that children make, but resolve to make choices with the intelligence—not the feelings.

# CHOICE AWARENESS

Make your children aware of the many choices that they have each day, and the importance of each of those choices. Some day they will be what they have chosen to be and ultimately they will have to be happy with the results of their choices. Tell them they have a free will to make whatever conscious choices they wish. All choices are made in the presence of God's love for them. God is sort of a cheerleader for their making wise choices because He loves them and wants the best for them. Allow children to make their own wise choices within a reasonable framework. We may not be aware of what God, in His infinite wisdom, has in store for them, and certainly we are not aware of unconscious influences. Our role is to commend them for using their intelligence in making their choices rather than acting out of feelings.

# RATIONAL DECISION-MAKING

The Help Sheet [*page 45*] provides a rational evaluation of behavior. Of major importance is helping children learn to claim responsibility for their choices of behavior (confession). The tendency is to blame other people, things, and circumstances for the results of unwise choices. Once they have placed the blame elsewhere, they feel no need to change their behavior.

They just continue to blame the world/others for their "misfortunes" without admitting that they have played a part in the cause of their misfortunes.

To facilitate wise decision-making, use the Help Sheet. Use it whenever unacceptable or persistent negative behaviors need attention. Keep these in your child's folder. They are valuable in helping you to know if your child is an angry child or a child needing attention, so keep a supply of Help Sheets available.

## HELP SHEET IN-DEPTH

1. *What did you choose to do?*
   - This is a confession for the child. He/she is accepting responsibility for his/her behavior.
   - Notice that the word "what" is used rather than "why."
   - We want to ask, "What are you doing?" not, "Why are you doing it?" As we have stated earlier, the real whys of our behavior often are not accessible to the conscious mind. Even if known, the child likely will project the reason onto someone or something else.
   - Our job is to point out the reality of what the child is doing now, not to search with him/her for a "why" so as to excuse the behavior and thus not change.

2. *What did this cause to happen?* (to you, to someone else, to family/friends)
   - This question gives awareness of the results of unwise choices. It asks children to think about what they are doing to themselves as well as others.

3. *Was it a wise choice?*
   - This requires an evaluation measured against the *wise choice* standard: "good for me and for the people around me."

4. *What would have been a wiser choice?*
   - This expands the child's ability to think of wise choices. Allow the child to think of the wise choice and then commend him/her for using his/her intelligence.

5. *When are you going to do this wiser choice?*
   - This requires a commitment of the will. If the child repeats the unwise choice at a later time, you can refer back to this commitment and ask again, "What do you *will* to do about this? Are you choosing to have me believe that you are going to make this wise choice now, yet you don't plan to do it? So when do you plan to make this wise choice?"

6. *What do you think the goal of your unwise choice was?*
   - This helps the child to delve into his/her unconscious "hidden agendas," to understand what is going on in his/her deepest self. Parents or teachers can know what needs this child has, and thus deal with him/her intelligently.
   - In Walton and Powers's *Winning Children Over*, Rudolf Dreikurs provides us with a set of underlying goals of misbehavior. For our purposes, we want to label these "goals of unwise choices." These goals are attention, power, revenge, and inadequacy.

     Dreikurs says, "The misbehavior of children can be dealt with intelligently when it is understood as being directed toward one of these goals," and that, "in one way or another whether we are successful at it or not, we behave in ways calculated to assure our movement toward one goal: to have a place and a feeling of significance among others."

7. *Did you remember that you are a special wonderful person? Do you know that God is there loving you even with your unwise choices?*
   - Ask the Angel of Courage to take your hand and guide you. (Courage is the ability to conquer fear or despair.)
   - This helps the child know that he/she is forgiven and supported with unconditional love and courage to pursue better choices in the future.

> **FOUR GOALS OF UNWISE CHOICES**
> 1. Attention
> 2. Power
> 3. Revenge
> 4. Inadequacy

## GOALS OF UNWISE CHOICES

Place this chart [*page 46*] in clear view so that as discussions concerning behavior surface, you can use this as a reference.

Francis Walton and Robert Powers speak of misbehavior [unwise choices] in their delightful book, *Winning Children Over*. On the following page is their explanation, which you might use to help the child learn more about him/herself and some of his/her hidden agendas.

## A CHILD CAN LEARN TO RECOGNIZE THE GOAL OF MISBEHAVIOR

A teacher or counselor may help a child to recognize the goal of his misbehavior either individually or in group discussion. It is absolutely essential that goal disclosure be done in a friendly way. If you are angry or upset, wait for another time and a better opportunity. Learning to use the following sequence has also been found to be very helpful:

1. *"Mary, do you know why you* (name specific misbehavior) *in class?"* (The child's response is almost universally the same: to say "No." In the rare case where the child may answer "Yes," his further efforts to explain himself are plainly inventions, and do not prevent the adult from proceeding with the questioning as outlined here.)

2. *"Could I tell you what I think?"* We are not indicting the child, but simply asking for his permission to give him our opinion. Invariably the child will say "Yes," as he is interested in what you will say.

3. [Attention Goal] *"Could it be that you think I won't notice you?"* (or whatever variation of the attention goal seems best to describe what the child is up to). *". . . that you want to keep me busy with you?" ". . . that you want us to look at you?"*

It is advisable for the teacher to begin with such a question, related to Goal One (Attention). If there is no response, or some perfunctory facsimile of agreement, the inquiry can proceed through the other goals as follows:

[Power Goal] *"Could it be that you want to show me that you can do what you want and no one can make you do anything?"*

[Revenge Goal] *"Could it be that you want to hurt me?"* (or perhaps hurt your peers).

[Inadequacy Goal] *"Could it be that you feel that you won't be able to do as well as you'd like to, so you'd rather not try at all?"* or *"Could it be that you would like to get people to let you alone?"*

When you are on the right track, you will be able to observe a Recognition Reflex on the child's face. This is a sudden smile, with direct eye contact, sometimes giving the appearance of an involuntary response that cannot be avoided. No further questioning is necessary. On the other hand, if you have made a guess and you are wrong, you have at least learned that, and can proceed to check out the next of the goals. When you have a smile of recognition, or some sign of agreement, it will not be so easy for the child to continue his misbehavior. This is because he recognizes how he is contributing to his own difficulties, and he is aware that you, too, know the purpose of his behavior.

In the hands of a friendly adult this is a powerful technique. It is invariably encouraging to the child to discover that he is *understood*.

They go on to say that the above exchanges should "be followed by discussion of what you can do, together, to work out a way of changing the disturbing behavior." They caution us not to use these goals to label or accuse.

## SPECIAL WONDERFUL ME

> **SPECIAL WONDERFUL ME**
>
> 1. I have **_intelligence_** with which I can know wise from unwise.
> 2. I have a **_will_** or the determination to do what I know to be wise.
> 3. I have **_memory_** to look at the past.
> 4. I have **_feelings_** to enrich my life and to inform me.
> 5. I have an **_imagination_** to think of and create ideas — look to the future!

The Special Wonderful Me chart [*page 47*] serves as a constant reminder to the child of his/her spiritual make up/capacities and is used to point out the proper relationship between these five capabilities.

Say, "Because of the unstable nature of your *feelings*, you do not want to make choices based on how you feel (happy, sad, angry, afraid, hurt). Instead, you want to use your *intelligence* (what you believe to be wise) to make your choices. Use your *will*. Will to use your *intelligence* (not feelings) when making choices. Will determines your directions. If your will is in the right place, you will grow toward making wise choices."

"*Memory* will serve you best when you choose to remember happy, pleasant events. Of course, there is reason to think on unpleasant memories when that will help you to determine a better course for the future."

"*Imagination* is used when you envision the person that God will have you be and when creating possible choices for the future."

If you notice a child making what you believe to be an unwise choice, just point to your head (representing intelligence) and say, "Use your intelligence. *Will* to use your intelligence."

When you begin to use this plan, write out your *will* (what you want for that child or family). As an example, this chart [*page 48*] might be used in your home.

This chart will vary according to the place and situation. Place this in clear view. You will refer to it often.

> **FAMILY WILL FOR YOU:**
>
> You will learn all that you can this year about subject matter, about what your church teaches, about how to get along with others and have friends, about yourself, and how you can choose to have a happy and meaningful life.

You may ask children from time to time to write down their wills. "What do you really want for yourself this year?" "If your will is to keep the family in turmoil, etc., then our wills don't go together. This (point to chart) is your parents' will for you in the family. What is your will for you?"

## THE WHEEL OF MISERY

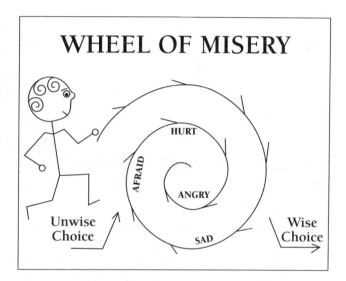

This is a wonderful tool for helping children understand that often they cause themselves continuing unpleasantness by making unwise choices and then refusing to make amends [*page 49*].

Explain that you get on this wheel of negative feelings by making unwise choices. Then things begin to go wrong. You are reprimanded by your parents, and other people respond to you in unkind ways. The result is that you feel hurt, angry, afraid, or sad. Chances are that you will make more unwise choices from these already unhappy feelings. Thus the wheel continues to turn, adding on more misery. In this willful situation you have chosen to be miserable or unhappy.

How do you get out of this miserable situation? You make a wise choice that might include an apology or saying that you were wrong. But don't look back at your misery. Always focus on choosing to do the kinds of things that are good for you and those around you. That way you will feel more the way you would like to feel. Again, you have a choice in how you feel. Friends, teachers, or parents do not control your feelings; you do by the choices you make.

## WORKING OUT CONFLICTS

Encourage children to work out their conflicts by communicating their feelings in the presence of their parent. Example: Jane tells her parent, "I don't want to sit by my brother any more because he is always making fun of me." The parent replies, "You feel hurt and angry because you don't like to have your brother say unkind things about you and you would like to move away from him." Jane's reply would be, "Yes and. . . ."

If at all possible, the parent would ask her brother to come and discuss this problem. Then the parent would say to Sam, "Jane has something she would like to say to you."

At this point, the parent instructs Jane to tell Sam how she feels. After Jane tells Sam, "I feel hurt and angry because I . . . ," the parent might say to Sam, "What did you choose to do or say that would have caused Jane to feel this way?" "What might have been a better choice?" "When are you going to do it?"

## WE BEGIN EACH DAY

Every morning, ask your children to stop, close their eyes, relax, and let their feelings float to the top. Ask "What are your feelings this morning?" [page 44] Say to yourself "I feel _____ because I _____." Suggest to them that perhaps they feel more than one feeling.

After having them decide how they feel, ask them to use their intelligence to think of some possible choices that might cause good things to happen in their lives, and thus help them to feel more the way they would like to feel. Encourage them to act on these better choices. They can improve how they feel.

> **MY FEELINGS**
>
> He gave me feelings
> 1. Happy
> 2. Sad
> 3. Angry
> 4. Afraid
> 5. Hurt
>
> I feel_____
> because I_____.

Add that there are a few things in life that cannot be changed; things that they really cannot do anything about, but they can change how they feel about them. They can try to let go and let God's love, peace, joy, and healing replace the bad feelings. "Let in the light of Christ." Remind them that they always have choices and that they can change how they feel in many instances.

The Good Life chart [page 50] also reaffirms the basic items in the *My Special Thoughts* book and should be placed on the wall permanently and repeated daily. This chart reinforces our goals. We tend to become that which we believe and say about ourselves every day. This furnishes the possibility or maybe the probability that children will become intelligent, reasoning, wise individuals who can deal with the problems and emotions of life in a sane and mature way independent of external direction. For the children, this chart (while knowing they are loved and accepted) might serve as their self-fulfilling prophecy.

**THE GOOD LIFE:**

I am intelligent.
I am wise.
I know how I feel.
I am able to tell others how I feel.
I picture in my mind God's special wonderful me, the person God will have me be.
Love, peace, joy, healing be in my heart today.

To summarize our daily routine:
- We check on our feelings.

- We use our intelligence to think of possible choices that would help us to feel better—that would help life to go better.
- We repeat what a wise choice is.
- We relate wise choices to intellect, will, and affections (feelings). In other words, we want to use our intelligence to make our choices rather than using our feelings.
- We repeat The Good Life chart and actually stop for a moment to picture in our minds the wonderful person God will have us be. We suggest to them that what God wants for us is so wonderful that we probably are not even able to imagine it.
- Repeat the family's will for them each day.
- Remind them that what happens to them is not as important in the future as what they choose to do about what happens. Use this concerning grades, papers, and such. "Our concern is not how many answers you missed. The important thing is what you choose to do about trying to learn those things that will help you to become all that you are able to become, all that God would like for you to become."

## START THE FAMILY PLAN

Make out a family plan with the children. Ask them what things they can do each day that will help the day to be a good day for the family. Write their ideas on a chart [*page 51*] that can be referred to daily, and evaluated once a week by asking "How are we doing?" "What can we do to improve our family life?" Then pray for help on these matters.

Once you list your family chores, you can use Post-It® notes with the various family names for easy changing.

Use Post-It® notes for the "Special areas that need improvement" section so you can change them easily each week.

> OUR FAMILY PLAN
>
> Daily Routine:
>
> Chores:
>
> Special areas that need improvement:

## ADDITIONAL ACTIVITIES FOR PARENTS AND TEACHERS

### SPECIAL WONDERFUL ME T-SHIRTS

Use a teddy bear or a large beautiful flower. Take a picture of the child's face with the bear/flower next to the chin.

Have these pictures developed at a camera shop or developing facility that can apply the picture to the front of a child's T-Shirt along with "Special Wonderful Me."

## Small Flower Pot Gifts

Paint the pots white. Let children paint or apply pink/red hearts along with a loving message: Special and Wonderful, I love you, God loves us, etc., for a Valentine gift or a Mother's Day gift. Of course, children can plant the pots with flowers grown by them.

## Dismissal

As often as is reasonable, line up your children at the door. Stand in the doorway and say to each one as he/she is leaving, "Tell me who you are." The child's response should be, "I am God's special wonderful person—God loves me."

Then give the child a cookie or small paper-wrapped piece of candy saying, "Yes, God loves you and I/we love you too." Give each one a hug.

## This Little Light of Mine

Trace each child. Put the pictures on the wall. Children learn the song "This Little Light of Mine," and then discuss ways that they can "let their lights shine." Make a list of the ways and place the list on each picture. Example: Do something nice or say something kind to Mother/Daddy/Grandparents. Do something kind for an elderly neighbor, etc. Make the list simple and specific. Check the list each week to see if they were able to follow through. Put a star by the items accomplished.

The Oracle at Delphi, the source of wisdom in ancient Greece, was inscribed "Know thyself." Serving as a loving facilitator and helping your children light their lamps of self-understanding and illumination so they can know themselves is truly a gift of love. An increased consciousness releases love, joy, and peace (the love of Christ) into their lives, averting the likelihood of sin. This is a gift to our children now and to their children in the years to come.

*"I am the light of the world: he that followeth me*
*shall not walk in darkness, but shall have the light of life."*
– John 8:12 (KJV)

# My Special Thoughts

Child's Name

# My Special Thoughts

picture of child's face

# Mother and Daddy love me.

[picture of child with parents]

# Mother loves me.

picture of child with mother

# Grandmother and Granddaddy love me.

[picture of child with grandparents]

loves
me.

picture of child with other

and

love me.

picture of child with others

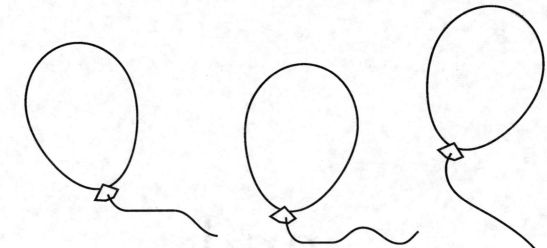

God made me to be His special, wonderful person. He will love me forever.

picture of child

# God gave me intelligence so I can know His truth. I can know wise from unwise.

picture of child pointing to head (intelligence)

I am wise:
I do the kinds of things that I know are good for me and for the people around me.

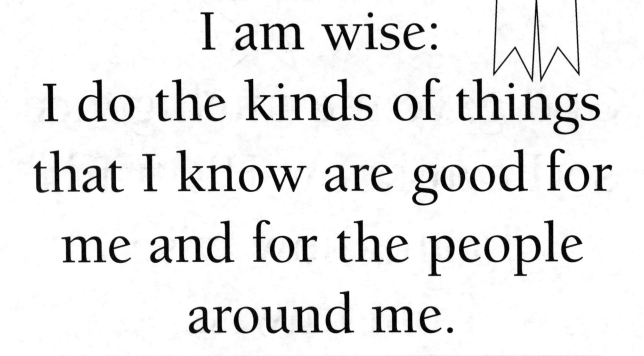
picture of child doing something helpful

# I know my feelings

- 🙂 Happy
- 🙁 Sad
- 😠 Angry
- 😨 Afraid
- 😢 Hurt

I can tell you how I feel.

# Today God loves me just the way I am.

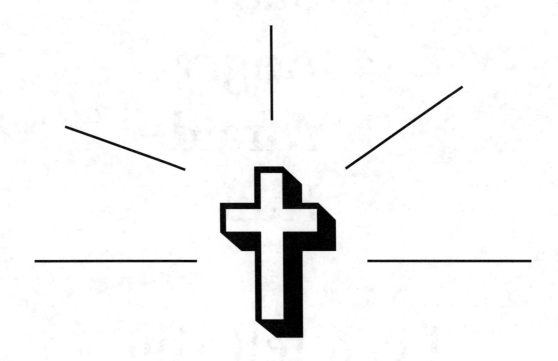

# Thanks be to God!

Now

- Love
- Peace
- Joy
- Healing

in my heart
so that I can be
the person
God wants me to be.

Angel of Courage
be by my side
today and always.

Now I close my eyes
and picture in my mind
God's special,
wonderful me–
the person God
will have me be. ✝

picture of child with eyes closed

God made me to be
His special, wonderful
person. He will love
me forever.

Name _____

He gave me Jesus in
my heart to pour out

- Love
- Peace
- Joy
- Healing

so that I can be
the person
God wants me to be.

## MY FEELINGS

He gave me feelings

1. Happy
2. Sad
3. Angry
4. Afraid
5. Hurt

I feel _____
because I _____.

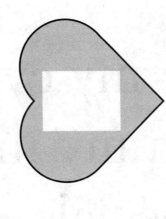

May
the Angel of Courage
take my hand.

God gave me intelligence
so I can know wise
from unwise.
I can know what
is good for me
and for the people
around me.

# WISE CHOICE

I do the kinds of things that I know are good for me and for the people around me.

# MY FEELINGS

He gave me feelings
- 1. Happy
- 2. Sad
- 3. Angry
- 4. Afraid
- 5. Hurt

I feel_____

because I_____.

Name _____ Date _____

# Help Sheet

What did you choose to do? _____
_____

What did this cause to happen? (to you, to someone else, to family/friend)

1. _____

2. _____

3. _____

Was it a wise choice? _____

What would have been a wiser choice? _____

When are you going to do this wiser choice? _____

What do you think the goal of your unwise choice was?

- Attention — "Look at me." ☐
- Revenge — "Want to hurt someone or get back at them." ☐
- Power — "You can't make me do anything." ☐
- Inadequacy — "Don't want to try because I might fail." ☐

Other _____

Did you remember that you are a special, wonderful person? _____

Do you know that God is there loving you even with your unwise choices? _____

Ask the Angel of Courage to take your hand and help you.

# FOUR GOALS OF UNWISE CHOICES

1. Attention
2. Power
3. Revenge
4. Inadequacy

# SPECIAL WONDERFUL ME

1. I have _**intelligence**_ with which I can know wise from unwise.
2. I have a _**will**_ or the determination to do what I know to be wise.
3. I have _**memory**_ to look at the past.
4. I have _**feelings**_ to enrich my life and to inform me.
5. I have an _**imagination**_ to think of and create ideas — look to the future!

# FAMILY WILL FOR YOU:

You will learn all that you can this year about subject matter, about what your church teaches, about how to get along with others and have friends, about yourself, and how you can choose to have a happy and meaningful life.

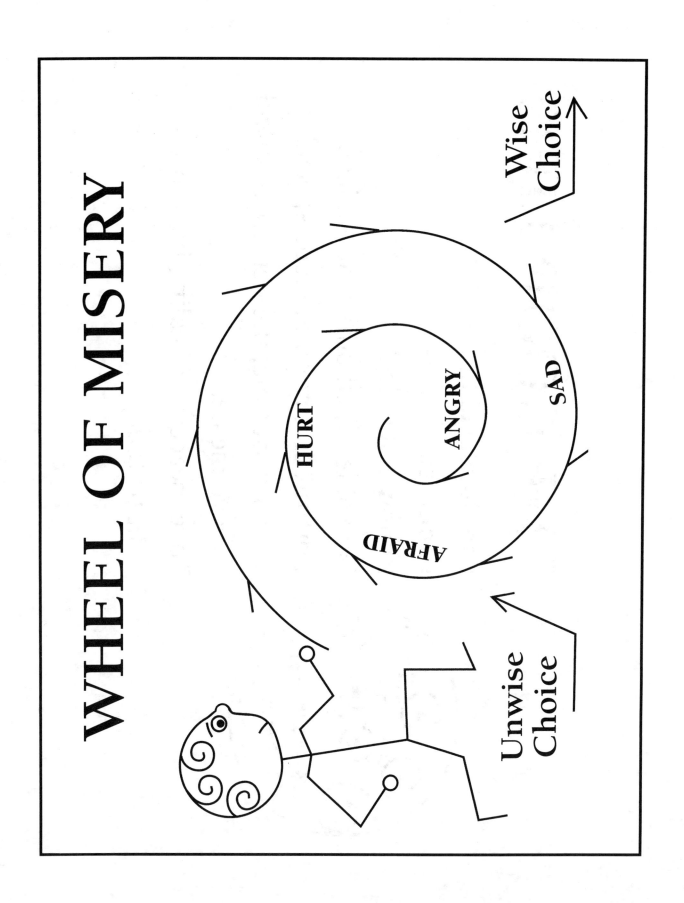

# THE GOOD LIFE:

I am intelligent.

I am wise.

I know how I feel.

I am able to tell others how I feel.

I picture in my mind God's special wonderful me, the person God will have me be.

Love, peace, joy, healing be in my heart today.

# OUR FAMILY PLAN

Daily Routine:

Chores:

Special areas that need improvement:

WONDERFUL PERSON!

God made me to be His special, wonderful person. He will love me forever.

# Bibliography

Jung, Carl. *Psychology and Religion: West and East*, vol. 11. The Collected Works of C. G. Jung, Bollingen series 20. Princeton, N.J.: Princeton University Press, 1969.

Keating, Thomas. *Invitation to Love: The Way of Christian Contemplation*. New York, N.Y.: The Continuum Publishing Co., 1992.

———. *The Better Part: Stages of Contemplative Living*. New York, N.Y.: Continuum Publishing Company, 1998.

Kelsey, Morton. *Discernment: A Study in Ecstasy and Evil*. New York, N.Y.: Paulist Press, 1978.

Rubin, Theodore. *Compassion and Self-Hate: An Alternative to Despair*. New York, N.Y.: Ballantine Books, 1975.

Sanford, John. *Healing Body and Soul: The Meaning of Illness in the New Testament and in Psychotherapy*. Louisville, Ky.: Westminster John Knox Press, 1992.

Walton, Francis and Robert Powers. *Winning Children Over: A Manual for Teachers, Counselors, Principals, and Parents*. N.p.: Practical Psychology Associates, 1974.